ALONG LIFE'S WAY

Edited by

Natalie Nightingale

First published in Great Britain in 2002 by
POETRY NOW
Remus House,
Coltsfoot Drive,
Peterborough, PE2 9JX
Telephone (01733) 898101
Fax (01733) 313524

HB ISBN 0 75434 361 8
SB ISBN 0 75434 362 6

FOREWORD

Although we are a nation of poets we are accused of not reading poetry, or buying poetry books. After many years of listening to the incessant gripes of poetry publishers, I can only assume that the books they publish, in general, are books that most people do not want to read.

Poetry should not be obscure, introverted, and as cryptic as a crossword puzzle: it is the poet's duty to reach out and embrace the world.

The world owes the poet nothing and we should not be expected to dig and delve into a rambling discourse searching for some inner meaning.

The reason we write poetry (and almost all of us do) is because we want to communicate: an ideal; an idea; or a specific feeling. Poetry is as essential in communication, as a letter; a radio; a telephone, and the main criterion for selecting the poems in this anthology is very simple: they communicate.

CONTENTS

PINK . . .

I have a pink money pot . . .
You came bursting in
the door with it in your usual
ungracious, noisy way
a few weeks ago . . .
Bought you a brilliant present
you announced, grinning
all over your young face
beaming happiness all over the place . . .
It's a money pot . . .
It's pink, your favourite colour . . .
You can keep all your pound coins safe in it
    Smash when full . . . the label says
    Making a wish as you do
We can go on a spending spree
to buy shoes, silly hats, maybe even a tree . . .
Haven't got any money I chipped in
Don't have any coins to drop in
Could I keep my collection of smiles
happy times and kind words
in my pink money pot
Then when full
I can still smash and wish
We can still celebrate and buy a tree
good things will tumble out and be set free
and overwhelm me, making me smile
just like you always do every time you visit
    Smash when full the label says
    Making a wish as you do . . .

Netta Irvine

LOVE ON THE ROCKS

I'm trying not to move . . . complete devotion.
Clinging to this moment like a limpet
or a muscle at low tide -
letting juices trapped inside go deeper still
with each salt lick
and lapping motion . . .

There's an ocean yet to fathom -
but then I hear it; whispering - insistent,
'Maintain the flow . . don't lose momentum.'

Suddenly I'm terrified, but of what?
Fear the moon may shut her eyes,
- forget to tell the tides to swell
and swish me all about?
That I will be stranded, marooned -
stuck in this one spot forever.
Or some loving rock may turn into a sponge and suck me dry?

'Keep moving' - that voice again.
So I loosen my hold, head towards the shallows -
    and instantly, a swoop, a blur of feathers, light . . .
Now a golden scoop lifts me up, high into the clouds, then . . .

    Plop -
down I go, an everlasting drop, head first into the bucket.
Hell bent, spiralling towards the damp dark bottom.
Only my innocent tongue
clinging to the greased sides,
slowing the inevitable descent.

Later, at my consciousness-raising group,
after we have all had our moment -
I remark how there's a 'men' in mo*men*tum.
It's looking good till someone else points out
there's also a 'Mom' and a 'tum',
We all have a group hug.
Stay very still for a long time.

Pete Mullineaux

SNATCH

Years together in the same bed
Love sits up awake
Tapping its finger impatiently
On a matchbox waiting to burn

The screen window keeps out the moth
Away from morning's clothes
Which dance
Inside out skeletons
In the darkness

And you snatch her cigarettes
You snatch the invitations
Mid sentence, you snatch at interruptions
Only have one way conversations

As friends I never noticed
And I dreamed for what I thought I saw
And leaving the audience and taking my seat in your home
I wonder whom the act was for

Is it for you?
With the safety of a psycho king
Every gun at your command
Sir

There is a whisper of a mutiny you see
On every broken lip
On every drunken mind
There's a whisper of desertion
One day on waking
You might find yourself
Stripped and kneeled
Stretched out on the rack
Because when you say I love you
I've noticed that she doesn't say it back

Ben Cassidy

FLUORESCENT CLOUDS

Like a lion's mane summer tossed,
Like the yellow men line dancing
Marking silver trails on asphalt,
So advancing clouds are leading,
Crowning ancient willows
In the tarmac of the night.

Avoiding snail trails
Of torrent jets.
They, like traffic men,
Appear at night
Tinged by the falling sun
Yet darkly, suggest a marker for the shy,
A cloak to hide the vulnerability of the winter sky.

Diane Burrow

SOUND OF THUNDER

Thunder in the New York sky,
I can only hear the children cry.
Like autumn leaves they fall from
A great height,
Brave men weep at their terrible plight.

Mightily did the ground shake,
Fearfully did our hearts quake,
As those magical towers
Fell from sight.

All those who were loved,
The brave and the just,
Soared towards the heavens,
In a billowing cloud of dust.

Men of terror dance in glee,
The blackness of their souls
Bared for all to see.
Sons of Satan, your master awaits,
Not for you heaven's gate.

So many countries
Have joined the fight,
Soon you will discovery,
The might of the right.

J W Murison

THANKS PAL

Never answer when I call you, are you deaf or just don't care?
When I go to put my feet up guess who's sitting in my chair.
Always drooling when I'm cooking, always sniffing, always looking,
Fixing me with anxious stare.
Don't I feed you when you're hungry even when I do not eat?
Pangs of hunger always ail you, always hanging round my feet.
Always snatching what I'm dropping, munching, chewing,
never stopping,
Making sure that I'm aware.
'There's the dinner you are craving,' nose in bowl and tail a-waving,
Licking up the mat and flooring - No! There isn't any more.
Ah, at last your eyes are closing, in my way but softly dozing,
Ears a-twitching, face bewitching - why did I adopt this hound?
Yawning, scratching, fleas a-catching, muddy paws and tatty ears,
Big brown eyes with love are shining, never mind the barks
and whining.
Doesn't see the lines and greying, listens to each word I'm saying,
I'm so glad it's me you found.
Lonely till you came tail wagging, old and weary spirits sagging,
Conscious of my body aching, now my miseries forsaking,
'Walkies please,' all else ignoring, games of ball for the enjoying,
You have turned my life around.

S Baker

THE FLAME

Your existence is a sweet concoction of
Radiance into these lonely veins.
Your smile an instrument of
Wonder, flooding me the
Earth as if the rain.
You may have
Never seen
My face
Although
Somehow
I've felt your touch
And kissed the crippling
Heat of you the flame.

David Mensah

HELLO, HOW ARE YOU?

A familiar sound
like that special touch
greets a new day
embracing feelings and affection.
Cat lovers too
who commune with their pets
rather than seeing them simply as animals
recognise the personal bonds enjoyed.
A sense of caring
mutually shared.
Moments of extraordinary closeness
yet independence too.

Margaret Ann Wheatley

A DIFFERENT GAME

The crunch of stiff frost under foot,
heavily he treads,
surging forwards with each step,
pushing off either leg,
with actions louder than any words.
Houses like ghostly figures
drawn in pale ink line the distance
and mark the boundaries of this playing field,
their painted brick edges
merge with the greyness
and complete a dull, barren landscape.

Trees bear silent witness.
At some point in the not so different past,
a day or two at most,
there was the noise of activity,
children playing sport,
maybe a game of football, rugby perhaps.
Stud marks of leather boots
still gouge the earth
long after the final whistle,
but are now frozen over with ice.

The crunch of grass,
a solitary footstep in the early morning mist,
he practises alone now for the next match.
Out in all weathers,
if you want to succeed,
a scarf keeps out the chill,
a cotton training top the damp.
This is the life, for an athlete.

Breath starches the air,
leaves its trail like a light aircraft
buzzing overhead in a clear, blue sky.
The sportsman marks his territory
with his effort.
From a window nearby
an adolescent watches the scene
with amusement and shakes his head.
He turns back to the video screen
in front of him and starts playing again.
His is a very different game.

Andy Botterill

ABSURD

If you are good at English
And can juggle words,
Use highfaluting twaddle
Which is usually absurd!
You might accuse a fisherman
For being cruel to fish,
Or huntsmen killing vermin
Or anything they wish!

The early bird catches a worm
But that will be taboo,
It will have to quickly learn
It's no longer the thing to do.
One's charming little kitten
Will grow to be a cat,
But it will be forbidden
To catch a bird or rat.
The very fact it's natural
For cats to do just that,
Is no excuse when simple minds
Legislate a crazy act.

You must not kill a blow fly,
Hornet, wasp or bee,
You must let them pass you by
And stop all life you see -
From killing to survive.
You must make them suffer
Who then should be alive!

You may be good at English
And can juggle words,
But try and use commonsense
Don't be grossly absurd.

D R Thomas

ST GEORGE'S DAY, 23RD APRIL

St George's Day - I have no rose
Proudly to wear, surpassing those,
The flowers of Andrew, Patrick, David,
Emblems on other hearts engraved.
Thistle and shamrock, daffodil,
Tell of the saints we honour still.
Andrew who fished the inland sea
Followed his Lord most joyfully.
Patrick enslaved in early youth
Still to his captors brought the truth.
David who followed Patrick's lead
To heathen Celts taught life indeed.

So what of George? In early days
He, dauntless, spoke in Jesus' praise.
Sometime in the third century
At Lydda died, undoubtedly.
The tale of the dragon which he fought
And Princess Sabra safety brought,
Depicts how Christians heroes' life
With good over evil conquered strife.
They say Crusaders won his aid,
The Conqueror's son his word obeyed,
And from that time good Englishmen
Shouting his name would charge again.
Edward the Third of 'Garter' fame
St George as Patron Saint would claim,
And down the years, so history shows,
We've worn on St George's Day a rose;
And roses in our hearts we'll grow
And praise St George, whose fame we know.

Kathleen M Hatton

THE WEREWOLF AND HER LOVER

She stepped outside,
Clutching herself,
From loneliness as much as cold.

She stared up at the moon,
And howled out her pain,
Why had he left so soon?

She felt tears burn her eyes,
Her heart felt torn open,
She would never feel his warmth again.

She wanted one more night,
To fall asleep against him,
To feel his hand on her.

She lay in bed,
Unable to sleep,
Caressing the spot he'd slept in.

She felt cold and used,
Hated him and yet loved him,
Why had he left so soon?

She knew he left because she was a wolf,
A creature that inspired fear,
Yet she was not evil.

She thought he would understand,
When they met he was void of preconceptions,
A man willing to accept anything.

She'd opened up her soul to him,
Let him see who she was,
And he had ran.

Aaron Rowinski

UNITY OF TIME

The fabric of undulating, sweeping gossamer
Throughout consciousness
Curving and arching it holds a planar shape
Outstretched the hand of time
And in my mind a sense appears
Holding on the grand design
A thought of impulse begun and gone
Holds more realism than ages past
Who could have guessed of such a thing
An interwoven dimension of solitary intent

Jennifer Cook

I WISH

Your childhood's gone
It's far behind
And the only thing that lingers
In your mind
Is regret

A Barrett

NIGHT GUARD

I am in my room watching myself.
Not asleep, I'm lying on my bed.
Mumbling nonsensical words, speaking
Again to the voices in my head.

It's strange that - watching yourself, I mean -
A form of madness that won't go away.
Out of body, in insomnia's hard,
Tight grip, awaiting the coming of day.

The rain is pummelling at my window,
But in here it's warm, I'm safe and calm.
As long as I am here to watch and protect
Me, the voices, the shadows can't harm.

I look peaceful now. Unmoving, quietly
Breathing. Time stands still in my twilight zone.
Insane? Perhaps, but the bond can't be
Broken . . . the two of us are alone.

Between myself and this girl on my bed
There's love. Yes: I think she'll be all right
Now the light's coming up, the dark is gone,
I'll return to protect tomorrow night.

And sometimes I really believe I'm crazy,
When the sun goes down and the mask comes off.
When I slip from my body and take my
Nightly post, and simply, carefully, watch.

Christina Comben

HOPE

In a world where the structures oscillate
in a world where nothing has shape
the nucleus - the fundamental structure
should be everything for us
I entered this acerb fight
that kills principles and prejudices
and where everything has gained a new value
and the goal has the preciseness of a laser blade
I forgot there was hope
I forgot there was dream
I forgot there was a cry in the night
Forgetting - perfect mask choking the memory
Time steals our seconds
like a thief lurking around an expensive jewellery
And we keep on walking
in the swamp of these adjacent worlds.

Maricela Suciu

THE OPPOSITE OF SOMETHING

What did I do this morning? Feeling all alone,
Well, I did - nothing.
Getting up and out of bed was all that I could take,
So, I did - nothing.
Just staring at these four drab walls, looking into space,
I thought of - nothing.
Summer sun or winter rain, it's all the same to me,
It just means - nothing.

Rodney Epstein

ONE TERRIBLE DAY

As dawn came up and lights went down,
The family rose and breakfast laid.
Each one needing something, even shared,
While father stood to pray to spirits all.
Shinto gives and Shinto helps,
Joined by sons who added phrases.
As each one gave their spirits praises,
The sun came up and gave good light.

People wending down the road,
As work was calling all to labour.
Yet as they walked a sound was heard.
Sounded like a hummingbird.
A giant bird of prey flew o'er,
Tho' no one saw what it left behind.
Suddenly there was such a flash, a bang,
The wind and then a hot blast came past.

When stillness and then the heat died down,
The smoke flattened ruins of a city found.
No soul stirred for many a mile,
The mushroom glowed and all life was drained.
Now naught was left, 'cept rocks and soil,
While people in the distance looked and watched.
Their city had sank in a brilliant glare,
And clouds of dust had covered the valley floor.

The bomb that dropped burnt all it touched,
As all before it turned to dust.
When the sun sank below the ground,
Spreading over it a long dark shroud.
Folding a dark blanket over the city,
Covering it all without a word.
Who to care can now be found,
To rise, once more . . .

Ken Copley

MORE

Sitting here wondering how life began,
What is our one purpose in life to conquer,
Have we already, unknowingly, unwittingly conquered it,
What about the others who with whom we do share this sphere,
The birds, the cats, the dogs, all animals, which roam,
The sharing of the pudding,
Is it done equally,
    Most probably not,
Do the others know about it,
    Most probably not,
And for the animals underground,
When they surface again,
    If they surface again,
What will they surface to find,
How will the human race come to an end,
'All good things must come to an end',
Who will be held responsible,
No one, as no one will be around.

Life, my friend is not only a question,
But an answer too . . .

Daniel Wright

THE PICTURE IS COMPLETE

The picture is complete, the two sides join.
Two halves of different worlds combine;
bringing opposition - unity of vision, not mind.

White turns to Black and says, 'I will love you 'til the end of time,'
and Black thinks, at least happiness is mine.

The two are one and seen as whole,
yet emptiness resides within the soul.
That which you do not own, you cannot attain;
acquisition is a blind man's game.
Pursuit of happiness an unskilful art,
remain at one, amidst the heart.

Light and shade, both which are true
brings no ease to either, in a parallax view.
No grey occurs in two perfected states,
division never does relate.
And so, they stay in 'wedded bliss'
the two not one of separateness.

Jennifer Cook

THE RETURN OF MY DAUGHTER

How I have longed for this day,
Months have passed since I have clasped,
Eyes on the jewel of my life,
And so I have received the news,
I have an overwhelming joy building inside me,
I picture the journey she's taking,
Her face is all I can see,
My one perfect creation in life,
I can feel her as the mileage lessens,
And my heart reaches out to touch her,
Oh how I have longed for this day,
Just to breathe her hair and know that she is there,
The most beautiful piece of me,
A child who's grown so sweet a personality,
Our phone calls have told me this is so,
Her hand again will fit with mine,
As together we shall make up for lost time,
I know she shall know me for I am her father,
My daughter, God how I've missed her,
In the perfect world we would be together,
But now for a time let the quality shine,
And again rekindle the bond we have,
As father and daughter.
My prayers have been answered
I can stand tall again as a man.
The parent thing is now at hand,
And I pray thanks to God,
For you couldn't have given me,
A better day.

Simon Fairs

FULL CIRCLE

A babe he was - too young to feed
Or care for his own infant body,
So hour-by-hour she cared for him
And kept him clean and sweet,
Fed him with food and love
She who gave him life
Gave him her devotion.

As time sped by he grew and changed
To toddler, schoolboy, stripling youth.
As manhood dawned he chose his mate,
A loving, caring bride.
He cherished her affection
As she cherished his.
He gave her his devotion.

The passing years brought slow decay,
The withering of youth and strength.
The fine young man at last laid low,
Beset by aching, weakened limbs,
By failing eyes, and nameless fears,
By swiftly fading memory,
And once again he was a babe.

A shell he is, too frail to feed
Or care for his own ageing body,
So day-by-day she cares for him
And keeps him clean and sweet,
Feeds him with food and love
She who is also ageing
Gives him her devotion.

Freda Knowles

EAST MEETS WEST

We're all there before the show
Ann and Janie, Linda, Bev and Mo
All the belly dancers, elegantly attired
Dressed up in style, music inspired
Then there's Tracey, Kay, Helen and Sue
All dressed in black as cowboys do
Hats perched on heads, full of zest
A unique dance, as East meets West
What the audience does not know
Are the nerves inside we must not show
Incontinence pants, secured in place
Toilets too far to save our grace
Rescue remedy, tonic or gin
That's the answer to our stage fright grin
In the wings, legs fixed to the ground
As the tension builds, the previous dance sounds
'Go for it, walk on now' they say
Why do my knees buckle that way?
What was the first step? How did it start?
Ah! There's the beat, oh no, that's my heart
Off we go strutting and swaying
Is it really so obvious we are all praying
Never again is what we always say
But you know, we really had fun that day
And as for stardom, well it can wait
We're off for a drink, 'cos we're in such a state

Sue Starling

HEARTACHE

In sympathy deep I send to you,
My very soul mourns your loss
Of innocents, too young to know
The perils of flight.

Fair hearts at rest,
Will always be,
Together in love and joy,
Happiness, eternal shall be thine.

Sleep gently young souls,
Our love is all yours,
We cherish you, every one,

But for you the lonely grave,
Together you are as one,
United in death, as you were
In life.

Jean Bald

So?

Droplets of crystal water,
cuts like glass,
through hills of brown smooth flesh,
the bone is exposed,
revealing rigid ribs,
a walking skeleton.

Chocolate and cream are but a dream to us,
we settle down to a lump less mess,
that slops onto chipped bowls,
our feast slides down easily,
but lumps form in my throat,
I gag and choke,
a shiver runs down my spine.

Heat burns me,
we pant like dogs,
but we do not wag our tails,
water flows,
but only from our eyes,
and all you can say is so!

Michelle Landon

THE QUESTION

Waiting
waiting
waiting
waiting
yes, it's this dull
and repetitive.

Time drags
like stone weights
across the floor.
It's my burden,
my struggle
but they feel it too
you can see it in their faces,
hear it in their words.

When?
The unasked question
the unanswered question
hangs in the air
part of our lives
for so long.

Katy Connell

COMMUNICATION

Where would we be without them
For we use them every day
We need them to communicate
Without them we'd have nothing to say

They're used to explain matters
To convey how things are done
To go into them and use them
I've found can be tremendous fun

They all have different meanings
To us they are a must
Without them we could not read or write
Which would be totally unjust

They're made up of different letters
We use twenty-six in all
You can write them, read them or speak them
There are millions to recall

There are short ones, there are long ones
Some are difficult to pronounce
We need a voice to use them
So we can give them lilt and bounce

We come into contact with them every day
They can be soft or spoken with force
We need them to explain what we have to say
You are right, they are words of course

J A Fox

SOMEDAY MINE

As much as I try, you pass me by
To my efforts you are blind.
Now I face sorrow, but I hope that tomorrow
Could make you someday mine.

Through autumn rain, the thought remains
Unanswered still through time
If times are bleak, perhaps next week
Would make you someday mine.

At times I wonder, through hail and thunder
If the sun will ever shine
But if there's reason, I'll wait next season
For you to be someday mine.

But now, instead, I look ahead
A few years down the line
And what's to say, one distant day
That you won't be someday mine?

Daniel Wakefield (16)

CONTROLLED WORLD

This beautiful world around us,
is so controlled and distorted.
Being lead by others who
    - don't really have a clue.
Yet by their actions and desires,
everything's distorted - even me and you.

Theirs is such a solid structure,
like laws carved in stone.
Their world means all,
devouring each and every soul.
There is nowhere to be or live,
or to survive - until,
their blessing is acquired.

But there is always - a way,
for their control to falter.
And so this control to sway,
trick is finding the method.
An endearing social play,
allowing us - to seize the day.

Gary J Finlay

SIXTEEN

Being sixteen was the worst time I have ever had,
Deep in emotions I couldn't reach a hand
With darkness all around,
In every little hole,
There was no single light to reach out to hold.
There was a time when I thought
I would die of the ache in my heart.
The ache that dragged me into the dark.
With darkness all around,
I could not get out.
Every door with light would close in my face.
The darkness went with time though,
Yet I thought it would never end,
But now I am really happy
That my life is at a mend.

Rashida Begum

THE TIGER AND THE LADY

The tiger paces his cage, his red-gold pelt
Restrained by regular stripes of sooty black
Lest his pulsing heart grow wilder still and melt
His frame entire with fire. He treads his track
Behind iron rods, in bars within bars. His paws
Descend in sequence, weighty, quiet, below
His massive head, whiskered with mighty jaws.
He moves along a beam from the amber glow
Of tiger's eyes, his shifting stare evading
Coincidence with mine. I long to feel
Our eye beams lock, to glimpse the spirit pervading
His powerful frame. Perhaps a look could seal
Some pact between tiger and woman? He will not spare
One glance at me, a vassal her lord ignores;
In his moving maze his gaze slices just air.
Time stretches out, I am held in an endless pause.
I must turn away, another failed endeavour,
For still he fails to notice I am here -
But all along he'd chosen now, not never:
He looks, impales me with an amber spear.
I stand amazed. What could that sharp glance mean?
'When a tiger regards you, you're marked as having been seen.'

S R Hawk'sbee

FELLING THE TREE

He struck the tree
With an axe
The blade sharp
Glistening
In the sunshine

It struck deep
And chippings
Spun freely
Into the soft
Summer air

A thud
Shook the earth
As the tree fell
Gracefully
Into a stack
Of timber

Death hovered
Menacingly
In the bark
Of that
Unsuspecting tree

Audrey Peteisen

FOOTSTEPS ON THE ROCKS

Guided by heaven-sent light
following your gracious will
to foreign shore far from sight
forsaking my birthright all.
Sea birds call across this golden shore
urging us across the waves
blessed be this little boat
protected is the sailor's oar.
Soft the grass of sweeping hill
as I lay my weary bones to rest
upon this spot your church to build
its walls a beacon to be blessed.
See the footsteps on the rocks
where sandaled feet did alight
in a sanctuary your spirit sought
to this far land safely brought.
Those born of proud warrior race
welcomed us with uncommon grace
like the wild goose with light descending
with praise our voices to you ascending.

Andrew P McIntyre

FIRST CONTACT

The air was scented, the car was rented
A faint hum of the engine, a drum of a bee's wing
The bee stung, the steering was slung
Out a tree sprung earth's lung
Shaking its bloom, a job for the broom
When petals hit metal yet the wood wouldn't budge
Glass smashed, a cymbal crashed
Natured clashed
A hymn was sung, a bell was rung
A harp was strung
The pollen counted, the pavement mounted
Just out for a drive, a visitor from a hive
No one survived.

Vann Scytere

DARKNESS

Stand a while with me in the darkness, stand by me . . . 'be steady
my friend.'
Watch the night descend like a mantel . . . it brings the day's pain
to an end.
Stand a while with me in the darkness . . . 'fear not for I am with you.'
See the trees silhouetted by lamplight . . . feel the chill of the
evening dew.
Stand a while with me in the darkness . . . see the world in stillness
of sleep.
As the cold wind whistles its melody . . . hear the child in the night
as it weeps.
Stand a while with me in the darkness . . . 'hold my hand I won't
leave you I'm here!'
Hear the night birds chatter their chorus . . . proclaiming that morning
is near.
Stand a while with me in the darkness . . . 'it's almost daylight
my friend,'
But unlike me, *You Can See,* and your darkness soon will end.

Laurence Eardley

REGISTRY OFFICE

I see plants springing new life
in my window box today.
In my patio wild woodbine grows
from strength to strength.

Walking along Grand Canal Street
I see couples preparing to take risks,
as they anchor their lives together
with signatures at the Registry Office.

Mary Guckian

I LOVED YOU SO

In a garden of remembrance
I stood beneath a tree
And gazed in fearful wonder
At the one nailed there for me
As I looked at that huge figure
The face, it seemed to be
Full of hurt and puzzlement
'Why did you do this thing to me?'

I stood there like a statue
As that face stared back at me
My head dropped down
In shame and sorrow
I could not say
'It was not me'
With heavy heart I turned away
All I could say was, 'This is me.'

One last look back before I go
And there I see what I did not before
A splash of red was on the ground
A rose - a poppy? I do not know
For me or not, I need to know
Again I looked up at that round face
And said to him, 'I loved you so.'

Opal Innsbruk

PASSING THROUGH

The streets were dark and narrow,
Buildings casting crazy shadows
Covering those who have been and gone,
Yet through the shadows people walk,
Unaware of those who walked beneath.

The buildings seem to want to say,
We long to tell you the happenings of those days
But over years we stand old and sinking
While new life breaks through what has been.

New life soon becomes the old,
'What mystery' no one ever knows,
Of how one comes but where doth go,
The shadows slowly drift away,
For the sun turns the corner about midday.

One cannot hear the whispering spirits
Voices millions in the air,
Left behind from bones that sleep,
So people rush around and live
The lives of those who now lay dead.

Oh, narrow streets again dark with shadows,
Hovering over unseen figures
What was their life and for what gain,
Years of sweat, toil and tears,
All will repeat itself through years,
While tall buildings lean and sink and listen.

Rosina M Drury

CRUISING

Cruising through suburbia
on my Italian thoroughbred
two wheeled dream machine
at the dead of night.

Man, alone with bike
and his thoughts
on the empty, lonely roads
what a wondrous sight.

Blip the throttle
what a glorious sound
a hundred horses
unleashed with venom and might.

The open road beckons
A fast twisting B road
that cuts through the countryside
the darkness, unmasked by my headlight.

Eyes reflect my light
from the roadside
probably cat or fox
frozen with fright.

I'll head back home
it's getting a bit fresh.
My gas tank is low
tomorrow I'll repeat the show
take the bike to the edge.
My mind's cool, my face is beaming, my knuckles are white.

Ian Mowatt

FAKING IT!

Are you faking it?
Are you taking it?
Wallow in your false glory
Living in your sci-fi story
Are you faking it?

Take it off the top shelf
Making way for someone else
Guarantee your number one
Opposition's on the run
Are you faking it?

So unreal, not the real deal
Underneath the covers
Soon to discover,
In your face, no disgrace!
Are you faking it?

But yourself a different look
Get yourself a nip and tuck
Hide behind a different you,
Inside it's the same old view
Are you faking it?

Dress it up in fancy clothes
Underneath no one knows,
What you're hiding,
Or disguising
Are you faking it?

Price it up with ninety-nine
Buy yourself a little time
You've been rumbled
Mustn't grumble
Are you faking it?

Paul Copestake

GIL 1942 MEMORIAL

We met on the train, in envy suits,
Soon to be in khaki, and Army boots.
Given a number, not called Mr,
Inquired of each other, if we had a sister.

Joined the same platoon, 1940 month of June,
Marched and drilled, chilled and marched,
Frozen in winter, summer parched.

Then, came the day of embarkation,
But to spoil our elation,
We went different ways.

Came, after many days, a letter from the Middle East,
I was thrilled to say the least.
Letters went, to and fro,
Spoke of spirits, high and low.
One day came a letter,
Marked 'Certified Deceased, Return to Sender'.

As I looked at the letter, I knew, unread,
I thought of my pal, on the desert 'dead'.
Memories of a guy full of life, and merry wit,
Always the same, fighting fit.

It is men like him, made 'Britain Great',
Bob, my pal, my mate.

J Knight

TRANSPARENT

I thought about true love today,
I saw her through the pane of our shuttered mind.

Then in flew a sweet, sweet bird
I somehow had seen before.
But she was beautiful and new
With a red, red rose
Tattooed on her right wing.

She sits on our shoulder
Speaking through our double-glazed thoughts.
Considering what could never be.

The window slammed shut
A little too quickly I think.

Now I'm trapped with something unknown.

A new start?
Perhaps if we all agree.

Soul?

Heart?

Benjamin Carr

VAMPIRE

I awaken; stretch my frozen limbs,
Embrace the darkness that surrounds me,
Disguising the malice of unseen whims
In the starkness that confounds me.
Within this cold and dusty tomb
I've lain at rest too long,
I yearn for those places where shadows loom
And the scent of fear is strong.
With a shaking, pale, translucent palm
I move aside more solid stone,
And leave my grave without a qualm,
In search of those who walk alone
On empty highways late at night;
Poor fools - no chance to hide or run,
For with my keen, unearthly sight,
I'll seek them slowly, one by one.
Seduce them with my scarlet lips,
Ensnare them like a clutching mire,
Caress their throats with fingertips
That tremble with a fierce desire -
A craving for that crimson wine,
That flows so deep through human veins,
Sweet whispered words, it shall be mine,
As biting deep, rich fluid drains,
Seeping through the punctured skin,
Spilling over parted lips,
Stained red with eager, wanton sin,
Intoxicating ruby drips.
Staring at the bloodless face,
I'll let the corpse slide to the ground
With unrepentant, evil grace -
Then glide away without a sound.

Sarah MacLennan

TENDRESSE EN HIVER

I hope, oh I do so much hope that you will be happy about it,
that, when you have time to spare from clever things, you will be happy
to realise that although through every moment and minute and month
and season and year that you have lived you have grown older,
you are not old.

The boundaries have been closing in constantly and consistently,
that is all and that is their problem, in no way yours.
You are unchanged;
a little altered, maybe, but unchanged.
You are still the you, you always were.

Nevertheless we, who have never met, must not meet ever.
That is as it should be.
You'd become bored with me, you'd find me trivial,
so I (merely a man) would blame you for rejection, not my own
                                                    shortcomings
and all between us would be spilled and spoiled.

Things are much best the way they are.
You can go on and on, writing the clever books you write so cleverly,
rejoicing in the fact that you're not old.
And I may muse and meditate, coax subtle sounds to sing -
sometimes to soar - because I am not old either.

Martin Summers

I FEEL SORRY FOR JAKE

It's been two years since you left me a note
You picked up your bag and grabbed your coat
Looked me straight in the eye
Walked straight past me, didn't say goodbye.

I feel sorry for Jake
He was only eight
How can a mother abandon her child
Guilty feelings till the day that she dies
You said you had no life
You said you needed space
Boyhood memories he has no trace.

He's ten today
Nothing from you for his birthday
He waited at the door
The postman knew what he was waiting for
Do you know what you have done
Poor boy, his life has just begun

Well it's been five years in June
He's nearly a teenager, time's gone so soon
In all this time you've spoke to him twice
Arrange to see him, you know it would be nice
He deserved better from you
You have so much catching up to do.

I'm so proud he's passed his last exam
He's turning into a clever young man
His girlfriend Nicole is ever so sweet
They keep telling me it's time I got on my feet
Not yet I'm staying on my own
Till my boy no longer needs me
And it's time for him to leave home.

Stephen A Owen

POEMS IN RETIREMENT

Written on a gloomy day

The time has come to pack my dreams away,
things I have longed to do but have not done,
places not visited, ambitions unfulfilled,
good that I might have done but did not do.

Days fall like autumn leaves
leaving life's branches bare,
and frosts of age have nipped
the buds where hope once swelled.

Beyond the mountains lies the Shangri-La
I never found. I shall not find it now.

Written when the sun shone

When I was young I had an eye to see
The wealth that each new day laid out for me,
From dawn's bright silver through to sunset's gold
And stars like jewels on night's curtain-fold.

Youth passed and, though the stars were just as bright,
I had no time to marvel at their light.
Glimpsed through a tangled growth of adult cares,
Earth's glory seemed to fade with passing years.

But now I'm old I've time again to see
The sunlight slanting through the apple tree,
And wander, dog at heel and stick in hand,
In wordless wonder through a moonlit land.

David Yarham

TROUGH BOWLAND AFTER FOOT AND MOUTH

Through the trough in winter go - as barren trees in moonlight glow,
Where sheep seek shelter from the snow - with the rabbit and its doe,
Unobserved by hungry foe - existing - waiting for the frost to go.

Soon winter's grip will be no more - and sheep will wander o'er
                                                    the moor,
As nature then will life restore - the grass, the flowers, the sycamore,
And newborn lambs will then explore - as melting snow builds
                                                    rivers roar.

Alas poor Carol will not see - our sheep and lambs from virus free,
Our ants and birds or bumblebees - horses, cows she will not see,
For then in southern parts she'll be - with just a fleeting memory.

D J Holt

HAPPINESS

Hollow footsteps resounding on the wet road,
People in houses feeling warmed that they are inside,
Cold fingers, cold face breathing in crisp air,
A man walking his dog and a cyclist - the only passers-by,
A mutual nod between them, a knowing happiness at being alone,
Seeing every leaf, every slight movement.
Things that are real, things that matter,
Into the wood, into the thickness of the trees,
Treading almost silent onto a change of surface,
A change of speed needed to cover more ground,
Leaving behind a heavier imprint.
The damp emphasising the real silence,
Seeping into the earth's core,
Into the soft fabric of clothing,
Giving a certain warmness to the atmosphere,
A certain feeling of peace.
Problems long forgotten, but must press on,
Now well away from the suburbs,
Timing must be perfected to make it home,
Before the darkness creeps in to make them unseen.

A Chamberlain

THE GIFT OF LIFE

Life is a priceless gift
With an unknown time span,
Mapped out, awaiting fate.
A journey down a path
With cross-roads a plenty.
It matters not what choice you make,
Destiny has already selected the route.
Mishaps and misfortunes are there to be dodged.
Precious moments credited along the way.
At the final cross-roads
You make your choice.
Renounce the devil and take your place,
Or feel the heat of all your sins.

Annette Murphy

OLD AGE - THE MOMENT OF TRUTH

Was it for this that I bore you -
And nurtured and loved you in youth?
Supporting in sickness and trouble,
This then is my moment of truth.

Your daughter I cared for and cherished,
Till speeding time bore her away,
With the loss of your father, I faltered,
Age's limits were ending my day.

No longer can I serve your purpose,
To tidy and clean in your home,
Duty dead - I am turned from among you,
And I am left desolate - alone.

My hearth and home were wrest from me.
E'en the house that enfolded my life,
And each memoried trinket and treasure
Of the joys, the grief and the strife.

Now I know that my uses are over,
Here I sit - in a home - mind bereft.
I have nothing more to do with life -
And I pray God will give to me death!

Peggy Sinclair

CAPPUCCINO TALK

Sitting over cappuccinos,
Trading tastes of sinful delights,
I'd look into your face
Searching for some ray of light.
Suddenly I'd want to stroke your hand
And say that all was well,
But sitting, sipping coffee,
Our distance only deepened,
Drawn from a similar well.

The aching grew in my heart,
My furtive desire to tell
That I knew exactly how you felt;
But your glazed eyes
Warned me always:
In that place do not dwell.
So I'd eat the sugar first
You the foamy bit last,
And from such simple gestures
A slight but subtle contrast:
I desiring an immediate resolution,
You too entrenched by sixty years
To ever ponder a solution.

Mother and daughter,
Coffee and chatter,
Nonsense, froth and laughter,
But, sadly, emptiness after.
Thus a possible truth between us -
An intimate bond to share -
Is layer by layer smoothed over
Like sedimentary rock,
Like cappuccino talk.

Pamela Bakker

GLENIS

So pensive she sighs
Those big brown eyes,
Wells of intricate thought.
Patterns and change
Life re-arranged,
Many lessons
Both learnt and taught.
Friends united
In life's passage to share,
And always knowing
That she will be there.
Friendship for joy and pain
Maybe sorrow,
Friendship for laughter
And clothes to borrow.
Cherish that bond
And grow in the knowledge,
That life's an education
And we share the same college.

Sue Umanski

BEING ME?

I hope that someday I will be me.
At the moment I'm someone I don't want to be.
I feel so alone. Life's so unfair.
No one cares for me. No one's there.
I'm alright. I'm OK.
That's what I say,
But it's not me.
Not I, but they can't see
The true person hidden inside.
I wouldn't be surprised if that person has died.
I hope some day that I will be me.
Someday, somehow, I will be free.

Dominique Braybrooks (14)

ARCTIC BEAUTY

Bare rocks
Quilted with brilliant colours
And swathes of softest moss.
Seagulls and terns
Whirl and dive.
Geese fly overhead
In neat formation
Necks outstretched like arrows.
Towering glacial monuments rise
Piercing the bright blue canopy above
Laced with puffs of skuddng cloud.
The sea is calm and tranquil,
Icy, still,
Mirroring blobs of virgin white
Gliding silently.
Tinged with sunlight
The landscape basks
In a soft warm glow
From the rising sun.
Bare rocks
Quilted with brilliant colours
And swathes of softest moss.

Nina Woolf

THE FELT OF MAN

When love pierces your heart
Let it bleed
For you are the lucky one.

If love should shed a tear
Let her drown
Watching her struggle amidst black sapphire waves

If your lover should one night
Set foot in your soul
To breathe life into your heart
Let him find you

Let anticipation crush you
Let these moments caress you

Let love take you.

Gazala Rashid

THE ADVENTURES OF R-NELLIE (1)
THE BUILDING OF THE PYRAMIDS

Thi' stand there in Egypt
Like big Toblerones.
But 'ow did thi' build 'em,
W' aw them big stones.
Thi' put little 'uns ont' bottom
N't big 'uns on top.
But Abdul, the foreman
Wasn't on hop.
Thi' sent for R-Nellie,
R-Nellie coptor,
Thi' sent fer 't' perlize
'N' between 'em they stopped 'er.
Thi' wanted summert fert puzzle
Th'arkiogocal doctor.
So thi' sent for R-Nellie.
R-Nellie coptor.

Bill Brierley

THE HONOURABLE MEMBER

My name is Peter Puce
And I'm MP of Dunloose,
And I don't give a damn
What they say.
I sit on the front bench
Where there's always quite a stench
But I don't give a damn
What they say.

There's a campaign on the air
In the media, everywhere,
That wants me to declare
All my interests here and there,
It's really not quite fair,
But I don't give a damn
What they say.

I've issued writs in all directions,
Filed suits, made protestations,
In the meantime making sure
That my seat is quite secure,
By hiding every shred of proof
Underneath my cloven hoof,
Damn you all, damn you all,
Now I say.

William Asprey

FAILTRACK
(March 2002)

Déjà vous, shambles.
Running late.
Leaves on track.
Wrong type of snow.
This time it's Hatfield.
The litany is long.
Death on the line at
Ladbroke Grove.
Clapham, Harrow and Wealdstone.
Up front it's the Times crossword.
Pinstripes, briefcases, rolled umbrellas.
One more day.
On the frenetic roundabout.
Must get that portfolio out.
He's passed the indispensable test.
The driver's passed a red light
And its oblivion.
Soon they all come.
The great and the good.
The solemn faces,
The glib platitudes.
'Must never happen again.'
Public enquiry, Royal commission.
Fingers are pointed.
The train has stopped.
The buck has not.
In another age
Time and place.
Did Benito get it right?
He made the trains,
Run on time.
He had folk killed,
In Ethiopia aka Abyssinia.
But not on the rails.

He was dispatched and,
Ingloriously hung up by his heels.
And he made the trains,
Run on time.
Our fat cats,
Of the rail networks and
Our weasel wordsmiths,
Of the HSE and DOT,
Will never be hung.
For anything they have,
Or have not done.

Edward Fennell

AWAKE TO THE DARK

Awake to the dark,
feel the warmth of enclosure,
touch the lacquered oak,
to the left, to the right,
above and below.

A sharp fear burns the reality of certain death,
the coffin is yours but the time is wrong,
your breath is limited,
your tears moisten,
you panic,
you scream,
but alas my friend this is not a dream.

David Bilsborrow

DECEMBER MOON

Some say a new moon means trouble.
This blueness in the sky
Seems calm,
But the branches fragmenting
The silver sliver
Are dead,
Bared by the cruellest winds
Seen in almost a century.

This is the blue of dreams,
A silver girl
Frozen in a garden
With a broken sundial
Holding time, very still.

This is the blue of winter.
Soon the moon will glide
From the grip of the tree
To meet the evening star
Rising in the west,
Lighting the wold
As night clambers
Over the darkening hill,
Dragging her velvet cape
As she goes.

Jo Leak

SOMETHING IN THE CORNER

Suddenly turning, there, over there
Is it just a shadow, is there something . . .
No of course not, there can't be
I'm alone in this room
It's just the shadow of the broom
Why is it so chillingly cold?
I feel the touch of . . . no
This room is just full of cobwebs.
Was that a scratching in the corner?
This feeling of dread
I hope that's not the smell of something . . .
Dead.

Elizabeth Morton

ONE FOGGY NIGHT

The fog was thick that night
Like a blanket on the ground
The street lamp shed an eerie light
A strange stillness all around
Sounds came and went
But nothing there to see
I wished that someone else was out that night
I wished it wasn't me
I put my hand in front of my face
Was it there? I was not sure
I'd lost sight of my feet
A couple of streets before
The air became much colder
My eyelashes turned white
I turned a corner I half remembered
I saw a familiar light
I put my key inside the lock
And prayed that it would open
Then I got the biggest shock
'I told you not to go'
My Mother she had spoken.

L Doel

THE DARKNESS OF YOUR MIND

Deep in the darkness of your mind
Many strange things you will find
Colours you've never seen before,
Terror stalking at your door.

Remember when you were ten feet tall
Now you're feeling so very small
Run to the door that once was locked,
Should I go through or should I stop?

Deep in the darkness of your mind
Everything turns round and round
Laughing faces, unpleasant words
Left is right and up is down.

Hands reaching out holding me
Can't get loose, can't break free
Makes no difference how I try
The time has come, I'm going to die?

Now the darkness has gone
And I feel at ease
But it was hell,
Deep down inside of me!

Brendan G Ryan

EVENING TIME

Sitting down at the close of day
looking at a brass handle on the lounge door
moving downward on its own,
this continues for a period of time,
the lock and door handle were taken apart
and found to be in good working order,
the handle still moved by itself in the evenings,
whatever caused the events has gone away,
a thing in life still not explained.

G F Snook

GETTING TO KNOW YOU

All those years whilst you grew up.
Knowing you yet not knowing.
Wanting to yet letting other
pressures erode the time.
You in your glass bubble
and I in mine.

Then you went away - no tears;
rowing your boat; not rowing,
others had tight hold of your oars.
Nothing can bring back lost time.
You in your glass bubble
and I in mine.

Water has flowed under bridges,
gathering tears, hopes and dreams;
slicing time - it waits for no man.
Mercurial wastage, streams-flow
water under life's bridges
carried my tears
tightening the band of guilt
around my mind
for not having time
to get to know you.

Now we share a secret smile
and hope with each cautious step
new bridges we'll build to close gaps
and God has given us time
to break your glass bubble
and I mine.

Pearl Foy

GOLD AND SILVER

(Written for my dear friends Sue and Tony on the occasion of their first visit to Australia July 2001)

Today in the winter garden
A score of daffodils are blooming
Sun yellow trumpets
Warming the cold moist soil
Beneath our naked silver birch

Today in the summer sky
Silver wings speed towards tomorrow
Swallowing the seasons
As easily as
Amber in-flight drinks

Tonight in the winter house
Friendship will glow golden
As early blooming daffodils
And love will sprinkle
Silver stars
Across the southern night.

Sue Parritt

NIGHT DESCENDS OVER THE FOREST

Afternoon fades into dusk,
The wintry sun sets,
Its blood red colour diffusing
Through the evening sky,
Casting an unearthly light
Across the forest:
Shadows lengthen,
The quiet shouts aloud.
Occasionally a fleeting shadow
Flits above the trees.
Then a blood-curdling shriek
Rings out;
No matter, only a barn owl!
Suddenly fingers touch your face,
Your heart leaps,
Silly, only a leafy branch!
You stumble,
'Damn that pothole' cursing
You grope your way.
The leaves rustle in the wind,
A denizen of the night
Cries out;
The pale light of the moon
Picks out the treetops;
Truly
The night lives.

Rupert Smith

Just Another Rainy Day As The Trap Was Set

Here raining, onto the parched earth
From which the rain rolls off
Yet rivulets form, on the house roofs
And run down drains, guttering, and had for a thousand years
Quietly, ducted, watched by water rats,
Water, and then flurries of wind, and then light.

M Courtney Soper

MIRROR IMAGE/IMAGE MIRROR

Is life after death really a mystery?
You are born into this world with nowhere to hide
Is what is gone before really history?

Your life is somewhat of a symmetry
You question as you are carried along on life's ebbing tide
Is life after death really a mystery?

As your road through life is filled with uncertainty
You work very hard at keeping onside
Is what is gone before really history?

Through life's ups and downs you maintain your sanity
There is so much speculation you can never decide
Is life after death really a mystery?

Never knowing what is to your destiny
Life's begrudgers you continue to deride
Is what is gone before really history?

When on your deathbed what will be will be
Talk of the afterlife you try to avoid
Is life after death really a mystery?
Is what is gone before really history?

Teresa Kelly

VILLANELLE FOR PAST YEARS

We have cruised over corals, he
And I, each unaware their place
Could be in cold Norwegian sea
Or Scottish. (We? Forgive that 'we',
Such cheek!) In summer's brief embrace,
We have cruised over corals, he
Long since, I later. Two or three
Seals! - or Caprivi claiming space
Could be in cold Norwegian sea?

On short old film, a joy to see
A smile refresh the Kaiser's face;
We have cruised over corals, he
Boyish, engaging then, to be
Happy that white ship's track to trace
Could be in cold Norwegian sea.

Mock how he swam, just one arm free?
'Kladderadatsch', to its disgrace!
(We have cruised over corals). He
Could be in cold Norwegian sea.

Veronica M Brown

CASTANET

All daily things endure until past;
From birth onward to eternal life.
Whence comes the breaking of the cast.

Until that time which is the last,
Through happy time and strife,
All daily things endure until past.

Be it the wheel turns slow or fast,
Matters not what manner is rife.
Whence comes the breaking of the cast.

Life's whittled notches being fully amassed,
'Tis then scions play husband or wife.
All daily things endure until past.

Since I be no doubting iconclast,
My 'ave' will melodious be on fife.
Whence comes the breaking of the cast.

Earthly things now being surpassed,
No need the more for pen or knife.
All daily things endure until past,
Whence comes the breaking of the cast.

Elwyn Johnson

CREATION

I can see God's creation all around.
Where trees and flowers abound.
And love to listen to the birds' sweet sound.

The bees and spiders buzz about
And weave translucent webs, no doubt
In the distance I hear workmen shout.

When I contemplate the sea's great power
I take flight and begin to cower
From that wall of water high as a tower.

God sends the lightning flashing fast
It strikes the trees, I feel aghast
I hope it will soon be in the past.

Upon my back I lie
And gaze into sapphire sky
And marvel at the stars so high.

Upon the pale blue sky I trace
Perhaps the planets of another race
Who may rock the King of heaven in space.

Margaret Kelly

APPOINTMENT DIARY
(Tune - 24 Hours from Tulsa)

There is a lot of work to be done each day of the week
The weekend was happy for us
Busy, yet relaxing and
Variable, just the same way.
Oh! We have always 24 hours of Saturday
Ah! Monday morning
One day goes slowly, one fast
Tuesday morning races, slow afternoon
Wednesday standstill, time speeds after lunch
With mugs of tea
Thursday is normal, progressing, time goes by
And so we hurried up, slowed down, exercised and rested
Shared out, if we could, worked by ourselves
Friday, all done, have a break
As much in the time, good stopping place
Oh! We have weekends, 24 hours of Sunday
Ah! Only one day, all day to get it done
Time for chat, coffee and biscuits
Time moves on, no turning back
There is next week.

Sylvia Berwick

THE KISS

(Sung to the tune of 'Fade' by Staind)

You come to me
Feel your cold breath chilling me
I turn to face you but
Your eyes are dark and scaring me.

I'm being drawn towards your mouth
Teeth protruding like sharp knives
Hanging over your thin lips
Darkness growing tight around me.

I can see you now, your hair shines
In the glimmer of the soft moonlight
There's a deep mist over the fields now
I can see it from my cold window
The chill of the wind excites me
Feels like your breath, haunting me.

Can I see your face?
I know you're beautiful, can tell by your kiss
Even if you don't do this for me
I will still love you 'til the day I die.

My memories were never meant to fade

Gemma Stothard

BLOODLINE

When fortune fails and hope sinks low
But Saxon blood is running true
There stands no fiercer friend nor foe.

Such men will neither weep nor crow.
They do only what they have to do
When fortune fails and hope sinks low.

In the deepest tragedy and woe
Here is one who'll stand by you.
There is no fiercer friend nor foe.

Such men stay when others go.
They are there and stick like glue
When fortune fails and hope is low.

They will not flee from curse or blow,
For the Saxons were a stubborn crew.
There is no fiercer friend nor foe.

Fear not, when beset and troubles grow.
Saxon blood will see you through.
When fortune fails and hope sinks low
There is no fiercer friend nor foe.

R L Cooper

THE ENIGMA

Let the stars rain down to a glistening light:
Sparkling like diamonds, fire in the sky,
Elucidate the owl on its audacious flight.

The moon embraces the wind that sweeps the kite,
Glowing, flowing, like a rocket ship, fly.
Let the stars rain down to a glistening light.

Its beauty colliding with the wintry ambience of night:
The sun, so warm, disappears, let it die,
Elucidate the owl on its audacious flight.

Can the heavens abide? They just might,
And if not, amid its allure, why does my satisfied heart sigh?
Let the stars rain down to a glistening light.

The sky's elegance, modesty is her plight,
She sanctifies the stars, so shy,
Elucidate the owl on its audacious flight.

Bursting flames, corrupting colours, dynamite:
The whirling comets, bustling milky ways, the magic of my eye.
Let the stars rain down to a glistening light,
Elucidate the owl on its audacious flight.

Paula O'Hare

INNOCENT WORDS

Innocent words from within, sighed:
Are thoughts wrested from afar?
The answers must rest only in the mind.

My words may have lied,
To stay forever as a scar:
Innocent words from within sighed.

The questions on my lips have died,
As delicacy is guided by a star.
The answers must rest only in the mind.

My feelings insist on being kind
Always responding: mea culpa.
Innocent words from within sighed.

Words must be there to find
Hopes ever remaining ajar.
The answers must rest only in the mind.

Nothing must be so signed
That freedom is ever a bar.
Innocent words from within, sighed:
The answers must rest only in the mind.

Michael Fenton

GONE BUT NOT FORGOTTEN

Remember I watch over you,
I'm with you each and every day.
I can see everything you do.

Our love will be forever true,
And it will always be that way.
Remember I watch over you.

Initial sorrow is now through.
Your life continues day by day.
I can see everything you do.

In moments when you're feeling blue,
And grief is more than you can say,
Remember I watch over you.

It's time you found somebody new,
For that is what I hope and pray.
I can see everything you do.

Death cannot separate we two,
We'll meet again I know some day.
Remember I watch over you,
I can see everything you do.

Kaz

DREAMS OF CUMBRIA

Among those far green hills that stir my heart,
And fill my soul with pleasure,
Yet make my tears to fall whenever I depart,

I do not need a compass, nor yet a special chart.
It is for me to wander there and fill my hours of leisure,
Among those far green hills that stir my heart.

There roe deer hide and wagtails dart
And nothing can cause my displeasure,
Yet make my tears to fall whenever I depart.

There I have seen the adder creep, the leaping of a hart.
For me there is no finer place, no land so full of treasure.
Among those far green hills that stir my heart.

Oh that I could paint them, but I do not have the art.
Suffice that they are there for me and my so selfish pleasure,
Yet make my tears to fall whenever I depart.

By trickling becks in valleys, where deer do bound and start,
There do I find such happiness in double, triple measure.
Among those far green hills that stir my heart,
Yet make my tears to fall whenever I depart.

J M Stubington

MANY TIMES

As many times before
I've told thee of my love
No one could love thee more.

Please hear me I implore.
I beseech thee oh my love
As many times before
My soul awaits thy sweet succour.

I am lost without thy love
No one could love thee more.
I beg thee open heaven's door.

Take me to the stars above
As many times before
Lying here my heart so sore.

I hunger for thy love
No one could love thee more
For I am empty to the core.

Devoid of thy precious love
As many times before
No one could love thee more.

Keith Campbell

VILLANELLE

While the scarlet sky settles the horizon swell,
The storm subdued in silence and abatement,
With a sharpened rustle of leaves to dwell.

A million birds flutter by the golden well,
Let love come amongst wizened kings,
While the scarlet sky settles the horizon swell,

Down memories' lane, the midnight stars fell,
Where compassion's vibrations leave the heart,
With a sharpened rustle of leaves to dwell.

Let only the union of a lover's spirit tell,
Where harmony and truth remain within,
While the scarlet sky settles the horizon swell,

Dictatorial lessons of empathy and bells,
Eloped in a land of tranquillity and dreams,
With a sharpened rustle of leaves to dwell.

The golden emperor has spoken well,
When the summer tigress leaves to sing,
While the scarlet sky settles the horizon swell,
With a sharpened rustle of leaves to dwell.

James S Cameron

WAITING

I am fancy of blood and bone well sped.
Though years since I cried for vigour.
Passing time that took me from a bed.

Weary of petition still voids led,
To other thrusts of immortal rigor.
I am fancy of blood and bone well sped.

The route is adverse: hard so to shed,
The load that grows each hour bigger.
Passing time that took me from a bed.

In counterpart there lingers not the fled;
Essence sleeps where dreams did snigger.
I am fancy of blood and bone well sped.

There's dalliance now I did so lately dread;
A faint-hood that life was dour to figure.
Passing time that took me from a bed.

I'll yield now the words life never said;
Buried riddles from the gravest digger.
I am fancy of blood and bone well sped.
Passing time that took me from a bed.

Francis Mcdermott

VILLANELLE

Paradox is the cornerstone
To turn from space-time to time-space;
Which the pundits will not condone.

Quantum activity alone
Allows time to tick-tock apace.
Paradox is the cornerstone.

Such logic is hardly their own;
To build on it is a disgrace,
Which the pundits will not condone.

Their objection cuts to the bone,
Although entirely out of place;
Paradox is the cornerstone.

The contradiction could be shown
Any fool's paradise to face,
Which the pundits will not condone.

Despite everything so far known;
It happens not to be the case.
Paradox is the cornerstone,
Which the pundits will not condone.

Ursula E K Light

WALKING MY DOG

Out to walk my dog can't now be,
Through pine woods along sandy paths,
On the way down to the empty shore.

He shared prime time with me,
Puppy scrambling, his barks, my laughs.
Out to walk my dog can't now be.

We walked as winter rain fell on me
And saw gentle spring's early daffs
On the way down to the empty shore.

Summer season, it was fun galore,
He tugged forward eagerly to waves and baths
Out to walk my dog can't now be.

Softy from my side away slipped he,
Old age stole the laughs, the baths, the daffs
On the way down to the empty shore.

Death can't plunder memory's rich store,
Nor erase from today yesterday's path.
Out to walk my dog can't now be,
On the way down to the empty shore.

Freda Grieve

GREAT SENSATION OF LOVE - LOVE ME DEEPLY

Great sensation of love,
You can feel its fantasy,
Love me deeply.

Nothing replaces love,
It's eternal love, eternal love!
Great sensation of love.

Mornings my heart,
Never stops eagerly beating,
Love me deeply.

Great love never dies,
Its warm sparkles,
Great sensation of love.

Kiss me sweet,
Don't let me wait,
Love me deeply.

Great love, great love,
Sparkles ever, never stops.
Great sensation of love,
Love me deeply.

Jalil Kasto

SPRING

Birds are singing in the trees
Branches swaying in the breeze
Spring's arrived - bad weather eased.

Crocus blooming showing their splendour
Snowdrops with their stems so tender
Daffodils in all their grandeur.

Tulips with their leaves unfurled
Dewdrops hang like tiny pearls
And God looks down on this His world.

One can only marvel at such magnificence
And be appreciative of all man's affluence
As we thank our Lord for his benevolence.

Cathleen Thomas

COLD SELLING

The stranger wore a tie of green
He beguiled us with a smile serene
That masked a man cold and mean.

He promised us a kind of heaven
He prefixed it with number seven
'A rosy cottage in the heart of Devon'.

Too late we learned his true intent
Nevertheless our money was spent
His job was done and off he went.

We went to see our dream-like dwelling
Its derelict air was very telling
Needless to say we'll be selling.

Jeannie Price

DOWN AND OUT

Mrs Pornoy is now prone to weep
When recalling not being discreet
With the young lodger who landed on both feet.

She was lonely you see, a widow too long
Who would often lust when on song
For that something she sensed very wrong.

Then she took in Claude who spoke good grammar
Had delicate hands and a gentle manner
Who in her works would prove a spanner.

Oh the thrill of the creaking stairs
The opening door, the prospect bared
And what Claude had Mrs Pornoy shared.

Then the fatal night when full of verve
He succumbed to that succulent urge
And went as he came during 'Soixante Neuf'.

T Cobley

SILVER ROBE, GOLDEN HAIR

Cold turret window veils the sun;
My life is waning, almost done.
I love the Queen - we both are young.

The silver is white, red turns to gold;
Her blue eyes sparkled, growing bold;
Our wildest hopes we would enfold.

Her ladies filled the bower with mirth -
Good, honest friends of matchless worth.
Brought mirror, comb, coals for the hearth.

But one grew jealous of the rest:-
'They make Your Grace a kind of jest,
A cuckold, Sire, I will attest.'

In pride we set our lances high.
The king fell first, we both must die,
No words, no salve, no peace to try.

They toll the bell. Let memories stay,
I wish her love and rainbow days.
My lily rose, I must away.

Brian Phillips

A BITTER BREAK UP

Do this, do that, like this, not like that
Oh! Why can't you just get off my back
Think, take time before launching an attack.

To break up is the only solution I can see
Face it, it's over between you and me
However sad and lonely that may be.

Have to accept it, have to stay strong
Don't let feelings evoke, times, they move on
Happiness and deep emotions have long since gone.

Young, early days of happiness and glad
Some of the best times that I ever had
So what did happen! Why did everything go bad?

Move on alone now before 'hate' sets in
Before memories get blackened, now that would be a sin
Feelings get crushed and become done in.

Start life anew, be strong, keep being true
Look at life different, without a rose-coloured hue
Ready to tackle anything . . . anything without you.

Susan Barker

STONE AND BONE

While walking on the shore alone
Where I am often wont to roam
I chanced upon a certain stone.

It brought to mind something I'd seen
In black and white on silver screen
Which wrenched from me a piercing scream.

Whereupon I felt a fool
On my first outing from new school
As those around me kept their cool.

For they all knew the script had planned
To show clasped in the actor's hand
What I had found within the sand.

A skull outlined upon my find
Looked just like Yorick, death defined
In Shakespeare's Hamlet - prose not rhymed!

As darkness fell I started home
And marvelled how both stone and bone
Could look the same in monochrome.

Paddy Jupp

LOCK UP YOUR GOATS!

A man rapidly making notes
Stares intently at my grazing goats.
His expression gloats.

They do not sense that he is near,
Engrossed in feeding they do not hear.
They sense no fear.

A young kid stands apart,
A sudden noise causes him to start.
My hand strays to my heart.

The stranger sits upon the stile,
I see his face break into a smile.
He will wait a while.

The kid forgets his kin,
I see the foreigner start to grin.
He desires the skin.

I wait and watch, body numb,
The youngster flees - still I am dumb.
He is saved from becoming an Irish drum.

Valerie Caine

BEAST

It hates me, I know; it's out of control.
It's heathen, it's vicious and has no soul.
Of health and patience, it's taken its toll.

When I switch on the power, it hisses and beeps.
It whizzes and chunters. It never sleeps
And refuses to give up the secrets it keeps.

It lurks on my desk, with malevolent eye
And - as through the day - I pass it by
It flashes and hisses a sibilant sigh.

I've threatened it daily and called it names
But it limits my access, despite all my pains
And still - in my office it evilly reigns.

It suffuses the screen with gobbledegook,
Then, when I try hard to locate my book,
It closes its eye and declines to look.

Since that thing arrived life's not been the same.
We stalk one another in a cat and mouse game.
But - admitted - without it, life'd be tame.

Joyce Dobson

NIGHT AND DAY

The daylight is so revealing,
As shadows, away are stealing.
That the darkness was concealing.

Now evening, twilight descending,
Roosting birds now are defending
Their perch, on branches unbending.

Ethereal light brightly gleams
As from the pure distant moonbeams
About the sea and land it streams.

Across the sky calmly drifting,
Backcloth of clouds ever shifting,
Mysterious, heart uplifting.

Creeping slowly comes the daylight,
As dawn takes over from the night
The darkness now has taken flight.

Meandering moon's near neighbour
Reigns supreme in golden grandeur,
Shines the sun in all its splendour.

Lilian Owen

FINE FEATHERS

Watching at the window through the pane we view
Birds dining at their table, in garb of gorgeous hue.
Although they wear it every day, it really looks brand new.

Phyllis Pheasant's frequently first, feathers frosted with the dew.
The robin in his ruddy vest is next to join the queue.
Squabbling sparrows circle in, as from the yew they flew.

Waddling on their legs so red, partridges, only two
Come cautiously, their painted eyes picked out in black and blue,
Watch warily, dab daintily, then suddenly 'adieu'.

Finches flit from feeder to feeder tipping them askew.
Nibbling nuts at rapid rate, filching quite a few.
Yellow-hammers, assorted tits, in colours bold and true.

Scores of strident starlings settle. What a noisy crew.
Gobbling greedily. Blackbird thinks, 'There's nothing left for you.'
But later on when he returns the pot's been filled anew.

We've watched them from the window all the winter through.
In rain and snow and shine they came and when the cold winds blew,
Making dark days brighter. Now we'd like to say thank you!

A Gwynn

VILLANELLE

Where thou art my heart shall be
O'er mountain tops, o'er land or sea
In fancy still I'll follow thee

The moonlit hours hold sweet memory
The fragrant dawn brings thoughts of thee
Where thou art my heart shall be

And if afar my footsteps roam
On wings of love tho' I cannot see
In fancy still I'll follow thee

Because you are so dear to me
My spirit still unfettered, free
Where thou art my heart shall be

Though separation may be our lot
This poem for you is 'forget-me-not'
In fancy still I'll follow thee

I love you now and shall forever
You may change but I shall never
Where thou art my heart shall be
In fancy still I'll follow thee

Norman S Brittain

CHEERS

let us all then agree,
to proclaim with great glee;
and applaud one two three.

hip hip hurrah,
hip hip hurrah;
hip hip hurrah.

and so we go on our way,
forth into the elated day;
light-hearted and outwardly gay.

so again hip hip hurrah,
hip hip hurrah;
hip hip hurrah.

but reality takes its toll,
as deeper issues begin to roll;
niggle first then pain the soul.

quieter pen hip hip hurrah,
hip hip hurrah;
hip hip hurrah.

time is the finemesh,
through which ideals fresh
have to stand the test and synchromesh.

hesitant then hip hip hurrah,
hip hip hurrah;
hip hip hurrah.

the truth that was yesterday,
is in the new moment of today;
and will be in tomorrow's day.

sober then the sung amen, hip hip hurrah,
hip hip hurrah;
hip hip hurrah.

Eric Ashwell

VILLANELLE

O Abelard, sweet Helöise,
Down through the years your story came
And which of us shall love as these?

They paid him teach her; he with ease
Had made his intellectual name,
O Abelard, sweet Helöise.

But each the other did so please
They lay and loved and knew no shame
And which of us shall love as these?

Men, vengeful, Abelard did seize
To punish, did his manhood maim,
O Abelard, sweet Helöise.

Condemned, on penitential knees,
They lived apart but loved the same
And which of us shall love as these?

Ask not, to educate or tease,
'And shall cold cloister quench that flame?'
O Abelard, sweet Helöise,
And which of us shall love as these?

Catherine Gregory

HOLY WRIT

Those zealots on Crusade or on Jihad
Present a pretty paradox gone mad,
An oxymoron that the good is bad.

The Scriptures and Koran, as leitmotif
Have tenets that instil the main belief
That of the virtues love remains the chief.

Incontrovertibly texts inculcate
That life is God's and so extrapolate
That killing one can never exculpate.

Through labyrinthine logic to a thesis
And tortuous twisting to a synthesis
They do apply their crooked exegesis.

So Gods of love and reconciliation
Supply distorted sham justification
For hatred and for mankind's alienation.

Patrick Brady